"These devotionals do exactly what they say on the tin! They are plain and simple, yet not dull or simplistic. These devotions are biblical and accessible, and I wholeheartedly recommend them to you. They fill a great need in the church for those who would love to know more about the Lord but maybe struggle with heavy reading."

Mez McConnell, Author, *The Least, the Last and the Lost*

"Chris's daily devotions do indeed explore the book of Jonah in a plain and simple format—they are wonderful! For those of us who find reading long, complicated books a challenge, these devotions are perfect. With a consistent structure that simply gets to the heart of the Bible passage, these reflections are laid out in an easy-to-read, clear format. They are truly accessible to all, and I would highly recommend them."

Pippa Cramer, MBE, Pastoral Care and Seniors Minister, Holy Trinity Church, Claygate

"At last, accessibility-sensitive discipleship materials that include all who seek a closer relationship with the Lord. No one should be excluded from spiritual growth or church life."

Dave Deuel, Senior Research Fellow Emeritus, The Joni Eareckson Tada Disability Research Center

"These *Plain and Simple Devotions* are very clear and concise daily Bible studies for people who find reading a challenge. I love the easy-to-read format, which makes the truth of the Bible accessible to everyone. The short Bible readings and simple structure provide a great way to encourage anyone to grow in faith. Chris has a gift for writing simply, and this feels like a valuable resource that will help many on their journey with Jesus."

Tim Wood, CEO, Through the Roof

"*Explore the Life of Jonah* proves that *simple* and *simplistic* are two very different concepts. Each daily devotional describes Jonah's experiences in clear language without sacrificing spiritual truths and depth. Questions encourage deep thought about the passages and God. Application of spiritual principles is guided by those questions. Each day's reading is appropriate for new or low-level adult readers. This book provides needed spiritual reading material for adult literacy ministries. I look forward to sharing this resource with such ministries."

Claudean Boatman, Coordinator,
SBC National Literacy Missions Partnership

Chris Dalton

Explore
the book of

Jonah

Plain & Simple
Devotions

Plain & Simple Devotions: Explore the Book of Jonah
© Chris Dalton, 2025

Published by:
The Good Book Company

thegoodbook.com | thegoodbook.co.uk
thegoodbook.com.au | thegoodbook.co.nz

A CIP catalogue record for this book is available from the British Library.

Design by André Parker

ISBN: 9781802542950 | JOB-008018 | Printed in India

Contents

Introduction

It is good to spend some time looking at the Bible each day,
so that you grow in your faith.
But it is not always easy to do this on your own.
Some people can read but don't like to 😕
Some people find it hard to finish long books with big words.
Some people find it hard to focus on long sentences.
If any of those feel familiar,
then these notes have been written for you!

A good habit

As we read the Bible, we see what God is really like
and how much He loves us.
So, it's really good to read the Bible every day.
It helps to find a time that suits you, and then stick with it!
Some people like to do this first thing in the morning.
Other people choose to do it in the evening or at bedtime.
Whatever works for you is fine. If you miss a day, don't worry!

All about Jonah

In this book we are going to read the true Bible story of Jonah.
Here is what happens in the story.

Jonah was a prophet who lived 2,800 years ago.

He came from Gath Hepher—you can see it on the map below.

God called Jonah to go to Nineveh,

a place where people were doing many evil things.

God told Jonah to give the people in Nineveh a warning:

God was going to judge the people of Nineveh

and punish them for all the evil things they were doing.

But Jonah didn't want to warn them, so he ran away!

He got onto a ship and went on a long sea journey.

He thought he could hide from God.

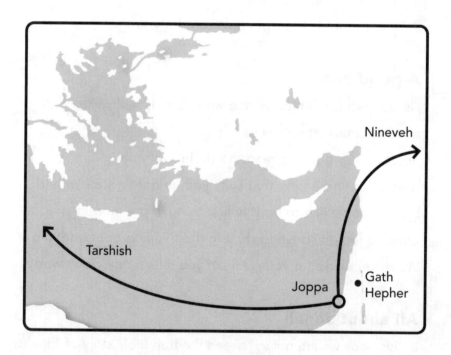

After a big storm and a 3-day visit to the inside of a fish,

Jonah changed his mind and went to Nineveh.

He warned the people and they repented.

This means they changed their minds

about what they were doing, and stopped doing it.

God saw they were really sorry, so he did not punish them.

He forgave them.

How this book works

We will look at a few Bible verses each day.

We'll think about what Jonah's story tells us about him

and what it tells us about God.

Then we will ask some questions

to see how it can challenge or comfort us.

Day 1   Jonah's past

2 Kings 14 verses 25-27

25 Jeroboam, the son of Jehoash,

made the borders of Israel

the same as they were before.

They reached from Lebo Hamath

all the way to the Dead Sea.

That's what the LORD, the God of Israel,

had said would happen. He had spoken that message

through his servant Jonah.

Jonah the prophet was the son of Amittai.

Jonah was from the town of Gath Hepher.

26 The LORD had seen

how much everyone in Israel was suffering.

It didn't matter whether they were slaves or free.

They didn't have anyone to help them ...

27 So he saved them by the hand of Jeroboam.

Some things to notice

This is the first time Jonah is written about in the Bible.

He's called God's servant.

He spoke to the people when God told him to.

God saw that the people were suffering.

He sent Jonah to tell them that He had a plan to help them.

The plan was to do with Jeroboam, the king of Israel.

God cares deeply about His people.

Jonah's message from God came true.

More info

When LORD is written like this, in capitals,

it always means God.

God is the LORD. That means He is powerful and in charge.

Lebo Hamath and the Dead Sea

were places at the edges of Israel.

Jonah was from the town of Gath Hepher.

That was in a region called Galilee.

Jesus came from there too!

Some questions to think about

- How do I think Jonah felt when God's word came true?
- What has God promised me that has already come true?
- Do I believe God cares deeply about me?
  What difference does it make?

Some words to pray

Loving Father, thank You that You care for us

and You work to bring about good things in our lives.

You are amazing.

Please speak to me and through me today.

Please help others to see how amazing You are.

I ask these things in Jesus' name. Amen.

Day 2   A message from God

Jonah 1 verses 1-2

1   A message from the LORD came to Jonah,

the son of Amittai.

The LORD said,

2   "Go to the great city of Nineveh.

Preach against it.

The sins of its people have come to my attention."

 Some things to notice

We don't find out much about Jonah in these verses,

just his name and his dad's name (Amittai).

God spoke to Jonah. He told him where to go,

and He told him what to do and say once he got there.

So far, Jonah had only given God's messages

to Jewish people. But Nineveh was not a Jewish city.

It was in Assyria, which is now Iraq.

What else can we notice from these two verses?

- God is called the LORD.
- God speaks to people.
- God sees all people everywhere.
- God hates sin. He wants sin to stop.

    (Sin means not doing things God's good way.)

That's quite a lot to think about!

It tells us so much about what God is like.

Some questions to think about

- How can it comfort me to know what God is like?

  How does it challenge me?

- If God is the LORD,

  then I should do what He says in the Bible. Do I?

- Do I want people to stop doing things

  that God says are bad?

  What about me?

  Am I ready to stop doing things that God says are bad?

Some words to pray

Loving Father, thank You that You are the LORD.

You have the right to say

what I should do and how I should act.

Please help me to hear from You,

listen to You and obey You.

Please help me to hate wrong things as much as You do.

Please use me to help others to see what You are like.

I need help to live for You,

so please fill me with Your Holy Spirit.

I ask these things in Jesus' name,

for my good and for Your glory. Amen.

Day 3   Jonah runs away

Jonah 1 verse 3

3   **But Jonah ran away from the L**ORD**.**

He headed for Tarshish.

So he went down to the port of Joppa.

There he found a ship that was going to Tarshish.

He paid the fare and went on board.

Then he sailed for Tarshish.

He was running away from the LORD**.**

 ## Some things to notice

We learn that Jonah didn't obey God.

He decided to run away.

His one thought was to get away from God.

Jonah went to Joppa,

which was enemy territory.

He got on a boat going in the opposite direction

to Nineveh. Instead of going north-east, he headed west.

It's strange that Jonah thought

that he could go anywhere without God.

In Jonah's time many people thought

that there were many "gods".

They thought each "god" only had power in one land.

Some questions to think about

- Do I ever try to "run away" from God or ignore Him? How?

- Do I believe God is everywhere?

  (The Bible says He is!)

  Is that a comfort or a threat to me? Why?

- What do I want to do about what I've learned today?

Some words to pray

Loving Father,

I'm sorry for the times I try to run away from You

or refuse to do the things You want me to do.

Please forgive me.

If there's something You want me to do today,

please help me to do it.

Please help me today to trust You more and to obey You.

Thank You that You are always with me,

wherever I am.

I need help to live for You,

so please fill me with Your Holy Spirit.

I ask these things in Jesus' name,

for my good and for Your glory. Amen.

Day 4   A wild storm

Jonah 1 verses 4-6

4   But the LORD sent a strong wind
over the Mediterranean Sea.
A wild storm came up.
It was so wild that the ship
was in danger of breaking apart.

5   All the sailors were afraid.
Each one cried out to his own god for help.
They threw the ship's contents into the sea.
They were trying to make the ship lighter.
But Jonah had gone below deck.
There he lay down and fell into a deep sleep.

6   The captain went down to him and said,
"How can you sleep?
Get up and call out to your god for help!
Maybe he'll pay attention to what's happening to us.
Then we won't die."

Some things to notice

We learn more about God's power in these verses.
He controls the weather!
God is in control of everything He has created.
But He has given free will to human beings.

What else can we notice?

The sailors had faith in the wrong thing.

The "gods" they prayed to had no power.

The sailors tried to save themselves.

They did everything they could, but it wasn't working.

Jonah didn't know about the problem,

or maybe he didn't care. He was asleep!

The captain knew that prayer was super important.

Some questions to think about

- What do the people I know believe in?
  How do they respond to scary situations?
- Is prayer important to me?
  How can it help when I'm scared?
- Is there someone I could offer to pray for today?

Some words to pray

Loving Father, thank You that You are so amazing.

Please help me to remember to pray

for all the people I know who are facing problems

or are trying to live without You.

Thank You for answering my prayers

in a way that is good for me

—even when it's not the answer I wanted.

I ask these things in Jesus' name,

for my good and for Your glory. Amen.

Day 5   Whose fault?

Jonah 1 verses 7-8

7   Here is what the sailors said to one another.

"Someone is to blame

for getting us into all this trouble.

Come. Let's cast lots to find out who it is."

So they did. And Jonah was picked.

8   They asked him,

"What terrible thing have you done

to bring all this trouble on us?"

Tell us. What do you do for a living?

Where do you come from?

What is your country?

What people do you belong to?"

Some things to notice

The crew knew someone was to blame

for what was happening. They were not wrong!

We don't know if Jonah was

the only passenger on board.

The sailors didn't know who was to blame,

so they cast lots.

The "lots" could have been sticks or stones.

They all picked a stick,

and whoever got the shortest was the loser.

Jonah was the loser.

So, the sailors decided that the storm was happening
because a god was angry with Jonah.

Maybe they thought that Jonah was a murderer.

Some questions to think about

- What was the terrible thing that Jonah had done?
- Is that what I consider the most terrible thing?
- How does this help me understand what sin is?
- Have I ever treated God the way Jonah did?
  How do I feel about that now?

Some words to pray

Loving Father, thank You that You are in charge of my life.

Thank You that whatever happens, I can trust You to help me.

I'm sorry for times when I disobey You

or try to live my life without You.

I'm sorry for times when I am cross and won't forgive others.

Please forgive me.

Help me to remember what my sin cost Jesus.

Thank You that because I trust in Jesus, I am forgiven.

Please help me to love others the way You do.

I need help to live for You,

so please fill me with Your Holy Spirit.

I ask these things in Jesus' name,

for my good and for Your glory. Amen.

Day 6 A big shock

Jonah 1 verses 9-10

9 He answered, "I'm a Hebrew. I worship the LORD.

He is the God of heaven.

He made the sea and the dry land."

10 They found out he was running away from the LORD.

That's because he had told them.

Then they became terrified. So they asked him,

"How could you do a thing like that?"

Some things to notice

What Jonah was saying wasn't the same as what he was doing.

He said he worshipped the LORD.

Worship means giving God His worth.

It's about respect, love and obedience.

Was Jonah showing respect, love and obedience to God?

No.

Maybe Jonah was relying on God's forgiveness.

In the past, he had seen God forgive His people.

The crew were really shocked by what Jonah had done.

They saw God's power, so it's no wonder they were afraid.

They thought that God was punishing Jonah.

Some questions to think about

- What do I believe about God?
  Does it match up with what I do?
- Worship is more than just singing on a Sunday.
  What else does worship include?
- Do I ever take God's forgiveness for granted?

 ## Some words to pray

Loving Father, thank You that You are my Creator.

You are both powerful and good.

Please forgive me when I don't act

as if I believe those things are true.

Please help me to be shocked by my own sin,

as much as I am shocked

when I see the wrong things other people do.

Please may my friends, family and people I work with

see that You are powerful and good

by the way I live and speak.

I need help to live for You,

so please fill me with Your Holy Spirit.

I ask these things in Jesus' name,

for my good and for Your glory. Amen.

Day 7 What next?

Jonah 1 verses 11-13

11 The sea was getting rougher and rougher.

So they asked him,

"What should we do to you to make the sea calm down?"

12 "Pick me up and throw me into the sea," he replied.

"Then it will become calm.

I know it's my fault

that this terrible storm has come on you."

13 But the men didn't do what he said.

Instead, they did their best to row back to land.

But they couldn't.

The sea got even rougher than before.

Some things to notice

Jonah knew it was his fault. He cared about the sailors
and told them to throw him overboard.
If Jonah wasn't on board, they would be safe.
Yet the sailors didn't want to kill Jonah.
They tried really hard to save themselves and him.
They couldn't, and things got worse.

More info

It's interesting that Jonah cared about the sailors.

Jonah didn't care about the people of Nineveh.
They weren't his people. The sailors weren't Jewish either,
but Jonah did care about them.

 ## Some questions to think about

- Who isn't mentioned in these verses
  but is really in charge?
- Am I surprised by the sailors' response to Jonah?
  Why, or why not?
- Do I ever act as if I can save other people by myself?
  How can I make sure I trust God to be their saviour?

 ## Some words to pray

Loving Father, help me to remember today that You are God.
Help me to be grateful that I'm not God!
Please help me to care about what happens to others
as much as I care about what happens to me…
or even more.
Please help me to be honest when something is my fault.
Please change me so I become more like Jesus every day.
I need help to live for You,
so please fill me with Your Holy Spirit.
I ask these things in Jesus' name,
for my good and for Your glory. Amen.

Day 8   Not guilty?

Jonah 1 verse 14

14 Then they cried out to the LORD.

They prayed,

"Please, LORD, don't let us die

for taking this man's life.

After all he might not be guilty

of doing anything wrong.

So don't hold us responsible for killing him.

LORD, you always do what you want to."

Some things to notice

As far as we know,

this was the first time the sailors prayed to the LORD.

It was a desperate prayer. It was a great prayer.

Perhaps Jonah told them that God is not just powerful.

God hates sin, but He also loves to forgive.

So the sailors asked God for mercy.

They knew that Jonah could die if they threw him overboard.

Then they would be murderers

and would deserve punishment.

Mercy is not getting the punishment we deserve.

More info

It's easy to get mixed up between God's mercy
and his grace.

Mercy is when God doesn't give us
a punishment we do deserve.

Grace is when God does give us
a blessing we don't deserve.

Some questions to think about

- Do I only pray when I am desperate?
- How and when has God shown me mercy?
- What do I really think God is like?

Some words to pray

Loving Father, thank You for the many times

when You've given me mercy and grace.

Thank You most of all for sending Jesus to die for me.

Thank You for giving me forgiveness.

I'm sorry for the times I think I can twist Your arm in prayer.

I'm sorry for times when I think

that You don't want to give me good gifts.

Thank You for Your Holy Spirit living in me.

I need His help to live for You.

Please help me to be kind to others,

because You have been so kind to me.

I ask these things in Jesus' name. Amen.

Day 9   Man overboard!

Jonah 1 verses 15-16

15   Then they took Jonah and threw him overboard.

     And the stormy sea became calm.

16   The men saw what had happened.

     Then they began to have great respect for the LORD.

     They offered a sacrifice to Him.

     And they made promises to Him.

 ### Some things to notice

The sailors received mercy when the sea calmed down.

It happened as soon as they threw Jonah overboard.

They knew that God did it. He answered their prayers.

Since the sea was calm,

that must mean that God was forgiving them.

Their response was to have great respect for God.

He was so powerful and so merciful!

They made promises to Him.

They responded well

to what they had learned about God.

Some questions to think about

- When has God surprised me with His mercy?
- Have I made any promises to God?
  Have I kept them?
- How can I show respect for God today?

Some words to pray

Loving Father,

thank You for Your love and kindness to me.

I'm sorry that I don't always show You love and respect.

I'm sorry for when I make promises that I can't or won't keep.

Please help me to grow in my love of You.

Please help me to trust You.

Please may my life point others

to You and Your mercy today.

I need help to live for You,

so please fill me with Your Holy Spirit.

I ask these things in Jesus' name,

for my good and for Your glory. Amen.

Day 10 Fish supper

Jonah 1 verse 17

17 Now the LORD sent a huge fish to swallow Jonah.

And Jonah was in the belly of the fish

for three days and three nights.

Some things to notice

God's timing is perfect.

The fish was there at exactly the right time.

If it came half an hour later, Jonah would have drowned.

God was in complete control.

Jonah didn't know what was going to happen.

But God had a plan to save him.

Jonah was kept safe inside the fish

for 3 days and nights.

He had lots of time to think about everything.

Some questions to think about

- Do I ever complain about God's timing?
- Which is better:

  God's opinion about when things should happen,

  or my opinion? Why?

- Looking back, can I see how God has used bad times

  to bring about good in my life?

Some words to pray

Loving Father, thank You so much for Your perfect timing.

Thank You for Your perfect plan for my life.

Thank You for the many times You save me from trouble

that I don't even know about.

Forgive me for moaning

as I wait to see answers to my prayers.

Please help me to be sure that You always do what's best.

I need help to live for You,

so please fill me with Your Holy Spirit.

I ask these things in Jesus' name,

for my good and for Your glory. Amen.

My thoughts and questions

My prayers and answers to prayer

Day 11 Help!

Jonah 2 verses 1-2

1 From inside the fish

Jonah prayed to the LORD his God.

2 He said,

"When I was in trouble, I called out to the LORD.

And he answered me.

When I was deep in the place of the dead,

I called out for help.

And you listened to my cry."

Some things to notice

Jonah remembered that before the fish swallowed him,

he prayed to God. He was desperate

and thought he was going to die.

He knew he couldn't save himself.

He had told the sailors that God created the seas.

Only God had the power to save Jonah.

But Jonah had run away from God.

Why would God save him?

Even so, Jonah trusted God

to answer his cry for help and save him.

Some questions to think about

- What's going on in my life
  that makes me want to cry out to God?
- How sure am I that He hears me
  and will answer me?
- God will help me even when I fail Him.
  How do I feel about that?

Some words to pray

Loving Father, thank You that You are trustworthy.

Thank You that You always hear me when I pray to You.

I'm sorry for times when prayer is a last resort for me.

Today I'm asking You to help me.

And please help these people too:

_____

_____

_____

Thank You for hearing me.

Please help me to watch out for Your answer

and to trust You while I wait.

I need help to live for You,

so please fill me with Your Holy Spirit.

I ask these things in Jesus' name,

for my good and for Your glory. Amen.

Day 12   Drowning

In today's passage, Jonah is praying to God inside the fish.

Jonah 2 verse 3

3   "You threw me deep into the Mediterranean Sea.

I was deep down in its waters.

They were all around me.

All your rolling waves

were sweeping over me."

Some things to notice

Jonah knew that he was in the sea

because God put him there.

Jonah knew that God was in control.

Jonah said, **"You threw me"**,

even though it was the sailors' hands

that tossed Jonah overboard.

Jonah said that the waves were God's waves.

Jonah knew God's power because of the waves.

He knew God's power in the deep waters.

Some questions to think about

- What does it mean to be sure that God is in control?
- Do I think that I'm where God has put me?
  What difference does it make to believe that?
- How might hard times help me to know God better?

Some words to pray

Loving Father,

Thank You that You are in charge of everything.

Thank You that this is true even when it doesn't look like it.

Thank You that You are with me, whatever happens today.

Please help me to trust You when life is hard.

Please help me to remember that You are always with me.

Please help me not to forget You when things are going well.

I need help to live for You,

so please fill me with Your Holy Spirit.

I ask these things in Jesus' name,

for my good and for Your glory. Amen.

Day 13   Certain hope

In today's passage, Jonah is praying to God inside the fish.

Jonah 2 verse 4

4   "I said, 'I have been driven away from you.
   But I will look again
   toward your holy temple in Jerusalem.'"

More info

God's temple was in Jerusalem.
The temple was the place where
people went to worship God.

Some things to notice

Jonah complained, **"I have been driven away"** from God.
But Jonah was the one who chose to run away from God!
He ignored that fact.
Jonah still had hope that God would save him.
He was sure that he would get back to dry land.
He was sure that he would look again towards Jerusalem.
Jonah really wanted to be able to go and worship God
in the temple again.
It seems that this was the most important thing to him
at this time.

Some questions to think about

- Is there something I've done
  that I'm choosing to ignore?
- When things go wrong,
  what do I think about or focus on?
- What is the most important thing or person in my life?
- Is there any way in which
  I need to look back to God again?

 Some words to pray

Loving Father,

I'm sorry for the times when I've refused to obey You.

I'm sorry for when I haven't wanted the things You want.

Thank You that in Jesus I can have hope.

Thank You that Jesus obeyed You always.

Thank You that He died in my place.

He was punished for my wrongdoing.

Thank You for Your forgiveness.

Thank You that I will never be condemned.

Help me to want to put You first always.

I need help to live for You,

so please fill me with Your Holy Spirit.

I ask these things in Jesus' name,

for my good and for Your glory. Amen.

Day 14   Saved

In today's passage, Jonah is praying to God inside the fish.

Jonah 2 verses 5-6

5   "I had almost drowned in the waves.

The deep waters were all around me.

Seaweed was wrapped around my head.

6   I sank down to the bottom of the mountains.

I thought I had died

and gone down into the grave for ever.

But you are the LORD my God.

You brought my life up

from the very edge of the pit of death."

Some things to notice

What Jonah said here sounds a bit like

some verses in the book of Psalms.

When King David faced difficulties, he wrote psalms.

They are in the Bible because God helped him write them.

In Psalm 18 verse 4 David wrote,

"The ropes of death were almost wrapped around me.

 A destroying flood swept over me."

Jonah knew the Psalms.

Jonah's words were similar to David's.

Jonah's prayer was based on God's Word.

He knew that he was in big trouble

and he couldn't save himself.

Jonah called out to God, who is the LORD. God rescued him.

Some questions to think about

- What verses do I know
  that remind me of God's goodness?
- Could I learn others... maybe Psalm 23?
- How can knowing God's Word help me pray?

Some words to pray

Loving Father, thank You for saving me.

Thank You that Jesus died in my place.

Thank You that nothing

can come between me and Your love for me.

Thank You that You are always with me.

Help me to remember that the problems I face

are never bigger than You.

Help me to trust You and talk to You.

Help me to remember all the other times when

You've helped me.

I need help to live for You,

so please fill me with Your Holy Spirit.

I ask these things in Jesus' name,

for my good and for Your glory. Amen.

Day 15   Just in time

In today's passage, Jonah is praying to God inside the fish.

Jonah 2 verse 7

7   "When my life was nearly over,

I remembered you, LORD.

My prayer rose up to you.

It reached you in your holy temple in heaven."

Some things to notice

Jonah waited until the last minute,

when his life was nearly over, to remember the LORD.

He didn't just remember that God existed.

He remembered that God was powerful to save.

Jonah was sure that God would hear and answer.

God was good to Jonah, even though Jonah ran away.

God sent the big fish to open its mouth and save Jonah,

even though Jonah refused to open his mouth

so that God could save others.

Some questions to think about

- Is prayer my first or last thought when things are hard? What about when things are easy?
- What gives me confidence that God hears and answers my prayers?
- Do I really want others to know how good God is?

Some words to pray

Loving Father,

Thank You that I can trust You to hear me and help me.

Please help me to remember to pray to You

when things are going well and when they are difficult.

I pray today for those who don't yet know You

as their good, loving Father.

Please use me today to point others to You.

Please make me brave enough to speak

and give me the words to say.

Please point people to Yourself through the way I live my life.

I need help to live for You,

so please fill me with Your Holy Spirit.

I ask these things in Jesus' name,

for my good and for Your glory. Amen.

Day 16   God saves

In today's passage, Jonah is praying to God inside the fish.

Jonah 2 verses 8-9

8   "Some people worship the worthless statues
of their gods.

They turn away from God's love for them.

9   But I will sacrifice a thank offering to you.

And I will shout with thankful praise.

I will do what I have promised.

I will say, 'Lᴏʀᴅ, you are the one who saves.' "

Some things to notice

Jonah knew that other "gods" weren't really gods at all.

Worshipping them was pointless.

Only God is worth worshipping.

But God loves even the people who turn away from him!

So Jonah planned to thank and praise God.

It seems that Jonah made promises to God.

Maybe he promised to tell the people in Nineveh,

"God saves".

Whatever his promise was, Jonah was determined to keep it.

He could only do that if he got out of the fish alive.

Jonah seemed sure that he would.

More info

In Jonah's time, people gave gifts of food to God.

They killed animals or gave part of their crops.

This is what Jonah meant when he said,

"I will sacrifice a thank offering."

Some questions to think about

- What do I think about those who have turned away
  from God's love?
  (This means anyone who is not a follower of Jesus.)
- How will knowing God loves them
  affect the way I think about them?
  Will it change the way I speak to them and about them?
- Do I think it's important to keep promises?

Some words to pray

Loving Father, it's so good that You love
everyone You have made.
Please help me to see people as You do and care about them.
Please help me with those I don't understand
or don't get on with.
Thank You that You are so patient and kind.
Thank You that You have been patient with me.
Sometimes I want to be more like You but sometimes I don't.
I'm sorry for times when I don't. I can't change on my own.
I need help to live for You. Amen.

My thoughts and questions

My prayers and answers to prayer

Day 17   Second chance

Jonah 2 verse 10 – 3 verse 2

10   The Lord gave the fish a command.

And it spit Jonah up onto dry land.

1   A message from the Lord came to Jonah

a second time.

The Lord said,

2   "Go to the great city of Nineveh.

Announce to its people the message I give you."

Some things to notice

God showed that He is the Creator.

He has the right to command creation!

The fish obeyed God and spat Jonah out.

The Lord also showed that He is

the God of second chances.

God didn't just save Jonah.

He gave him the same command as before.

The fish obeyed, but was Jonah going to obey?

More info

God called Nineveh **"the great city"** because it was big.

God didn't think it was great in other ways!

Some questions to think about

- God's power is awesome. What do I feel about that?
- God doesn't give up on us. When have I experienced that?
- Am I good at giving people second chances? Or do I give up on them?

Some words to pray

Loving Father,

Thank You that You don't give up on us.

Thank You that You haven't given up on me.

Thank You for Your amazing power and kindness.

The place where I live isn't great—just like Nineveh.

Lots of people don't know You as Saviour and LORD.

Please help me to pray for those I know.

Please help me to pray for my home town.

Please help me not to give up.

I need help to live for You,

so please fill me with Your Holy Spirit.

I ask these things in Jesus' name,

for my good and for Your glory. Amen.

Jonah 3 verses 3-4

3 Jonah obeyed the LORD. He went to Nineveh.

It was a very large city.

In fact, it took about three days to go through it.

4 Jonah began by going one whole day into the city.

As he went, he announced,

"In 40 days Nineveh will be destroyed."

Some things to notice

Nineveh was big. It took 3 whole days to walk across it!

Jonah took a whole day to get right into the heart of it.

He was probably smelly after being in the fish.

Maybe people found out what had happened to Jonah.

If that is true, then Jonah was a sign of God's mercy.

But Jonah's message was short.

It wasn't his job to argue or reason

with the people of Nineveh.

It was just to tell them the message.

What happened next was up to God and the people.

Would the people of Nineveh just laugh at Jonah

or run away from him?

Some questions to think about

- How confident am I about telling people about God?
- What are the most important things to say about Him? Could I sum up the message about Jesus in just a few words?
- God is in charge of what happens after I tell someone about Him. How do I feel about that?

Some words to pray

Loving Father, thank You for sending Jesus to save me.

Thank You that You love everyone

and You long to save them.

Please will You help me to share the good news?

I worry about saying the wrong thing and putting them off.

Thank You that their response isn't my responsibility.

Help me to trust You to be at work in them.

Please change the way they think about You.

I need help to live for You,

so please fill me with Your Holy Spirit.

I ask these things in Jesus' name,

for my good and for Your glory. Amen.

Change happens

Jonah 3 verse 5

5   The people of Nineveh believed God's warning.

So they decided not to eat any food for a while.

And all of them put on the rough clothing

people wear when they're sad.

That's what everyone did,

from the least important of them

to the most important.

Some things to notice

The people of Nineveh didn't laugh or run away.

They believed the message. WOW!

They decided they were in real danger.

They were sad,

so they dressed differently and stopped eating.

They wanted to make it really clear how they felt.

All of them repented.

To repent means to change your mind.

It means admitting that you've got it wrong.

It's choosing to accept the truth,

then choosing to turn away from sin

and go the other way.

It's saying that God is right and choosing His way.

Some questions to think about

- Am I surprised that this sinful city changed so quickly?
- What about me: what do I do
  when I realise I have been sinning?
- What could I do today to make a difference
  to people who don't know about Jesus yet?
  Will I pray and maybe also speak to others?

Some words to pray

Loving Father, wow, You're amazing!

You are so powerful and good and kind.

Thank You that You can change minds and hearts.

I'm sorry for the times I doubt that You can still do this.

Please grow my faith in You.

Please show me today where You are at work.

Thank You for changing people

and giving them new life in Jesus.

Please keep me praying for those I love and care about.

Please help me to show them how You are changing me.

I need help to live for You,

so please fill me with Your Holy Spirit.

I ask these things in Jesus' name

for my good and for Your glory. Amen.

Day 20   The king repents

Jonah 3 verse 6

6   Jonah's warning reached the king of Nineveh.

He got up from his throne.

He took off his royal robes.

He also dressed himself in the clothing of sadness.

And then he sat down in the dust.

Some things to notice

Nineveh was an important city in Assyria.

The "king" was most likely the city governor.

It's unlikely he was king of the whole Assyrian Empire.

But he was still very powerful!

He really believed that God could wipe out the city.

It's amazing that he believed God and acted as he did.

He took off his symbols of power and sat in the dust.

Some questions to think about

- What do I do when God challenges me?
  Do I ever think I am too important
  or too good to be challenged?
- The Bible tells me to pray for leaders,
  including church leaders and political leaders.
  Do I believe my prayers will make a difference?
- What could I pray for them?

Some words to pray

Loving Father, powerful God, no one is greater than You.

Thank You that the king of Nineveh believed that.

Thank You for the king of Nineveh's response.

I pray for those who have power in my city and my country.

Please show them the truth about Yourself.

Please lead them to turn to You and ask for Your wisdom.

Please help them to serve well for the good of all people.

Please help me to remember to pray for them.

I need help to live for You,

so please fill me with Your Holy Spirit.

I ask these things in Jesus' name,

for my good and for Your glory. Amen.

Day 21 Call to prayer

Jonah 3 verses 7-9

7   Here is the message he [the king] sent out

to the people of Nineveh.

"I and my nobles give this order.

Don't let people or animals taste anything.

That includes your herds and flocks.

People and animals must not eat or drink anything.

8   Let people and animals alike be covered

with the clothing of sadness.

All of you must call out to God with all your hearts.

Stop doing what is evil. Don't harm others.

9   Who knows? God might take pity on us.

He might not be angry with us anymore.

Then we won't die."

Some things to notice

The king knew that he and his people were doing evil things.

It was not surprising that God wanted to destroy them.

But Jonah's story proved

that God was kind as well as powerful.

The people probably heard his story

and saw (and smelled) the truth!

The king hoped that if the people changed their ways,

God would forgive them.

He told them to call out to God with all their hearts.
They had to concentrate so much on saying sorry to God,
they weren't even supposed to eat.

Some questions to think about

- Is there anything I need to say sorry to God for today?
- Is there anything I need to stop doing?
- Do I need to remind myself
  that God is powerful and kind? Romans 8 verse 1 says,
  "Those who belong to Christ Jesus
  are no longer under God's judgment".

Some words to pray

Loving Father, thank You for Jesus.
Thank You that because He took my place,
I am not condemned.
Please help me to hold on to that truth with joy.
Thank You that You are just and good.
You can't stand sin. I'm sorry for my wrong thinking
about You, and me, and others.
I'm sorry for wrong things I've done, especially…

_____

Thank You for forgiving me.
I ask these things in Jesus' name,
for my good and for Your glory. Amen.

Day 22   God answers prayer

Jonah 3 verse 10

10   God saw what they did.

He saw that they stopped doing what was evil.

So he took pity on them.

He didn't destroy them as he had said he would.

 ## Some things to notice

God can't change, because He's perfect.

He can't change, but the people did change!

They listened to what God said about them.

They stopped doing evil things.

They were no longer a people who had to be destroyed.

The threat of judgment caused them to change.

So God did not destroy the city.

How amazing that God reacted the way He did!

Some questions to think about

- How does God's mercy encourage me today?
- What would it mean if God could change?
  Why wouldn't that be good news?
- What is God's attitude towards people who sin?
  What about people who repent?
- Is there anything in my life that needs to change?

Some words to pray

Loving Father, thank You that You can't change, ever.

Thank You that this means I can trust You

to keep Your promises.

Thank You that You accept me just as I am.

Thank You that You will never reject me,

because Jesus died for me.

Please show me the things in my life that do need to change.

Please help me to see why they need to change.

Please help me to want them to change.

I need help to live for You,

so please fill me with Your Holy Spirit.

I ask these things in Jesus' name,

for my good and for Your glory. Amen.

My thoughts and questions

My prayers and answers to prayer

Day 23　Jonah is angry

Jonah 4 verses 1-3

1　But to Jonah this seemed very wrong.

He became angry.

2　He prayed to the LORD. Here is what Jonah said to him.

"LORD, isn't this exactly what I thought would happen

when I was still at home?

That is what I tried to prevent

by running away to Tarshish.

I knew that you are gracious. You are tender and kind.

You are slow to get angry. You are full of love.

You are a God who takes pity on people.

You don't want to destroy them.

3　LORD, take away my life. I'd rather die than live."

Some things to notice

Jonah knew that God was tender and kind and gracious.

That's why he ran away in the first place!

He didn't want the enemies of God's people to be saved.

He actively tried to prevent it.

Now that God was forgiving the people in Nineveh,

Jonah was furious!

He didn't think they deserved forgiveness.

Jonah experienced God's love and mercy.

Yet he didn't want others to experience God's mercy.

Before, Jonah didn't want to die.

But now he did—because God was kind to the Ninevites!

Some questions to think about

- If someone has hurt me or hurt others,
  do I want them to turn to God and be forgiven?
- Do I think everyone should get a second chance?
  Does God?
- Jonah says lots of things about what God is like.
  Which is the most important to me today?

Some words to pray

Loving Father,

help me to remember that Your kindness saved me.

I'm sorry for being angry

when You show kindness to people I don't like.

Please help me to want to be more like You.

Please help me to remember that all wrongdoing hurts You.

Please help me to be joyful

when people turn away from wrongdoing.

Please help me to pray for this to happen.

I need help to live for You,

so please fill me with Your Holy Spirit.

I ask these things in Jesus' name,

for my good and for Your glory. Amen.

Day 24   Waiting

Jonah 4 verses 4-5

4   But the LORD replied, "Is it right for you to be angry?"

5   Jonah had left the city.

He had sat down at a place east of it.

There he put some branches over his head.

He sat in their shade.

He waited to see what would happen to the city.

🐦 Some things to notice

Jonah left the city in a huff.

He decided to wait to see if God would destroy it.

East of Nineveh there were hills.

You could see the city from there.

Jonah knew all about God's mercy, because he had received it.

But now, God's mercy seemed to be

the cause of Jonah's anger.

Jonah put up a leafy shelter to give himself shade.

God asked Jonah whether he was right to be angry.

More info

Jonah's name means "dove".

He seemed more like a vulture waiting for its dinner...

Some questions to think about

- Do I think Jonah was right to be angry?
- What things about God's goodness give me joy?
  Do I ever feel angry with God instead?
- Am I like Jonah in any way?
  Or am I thankful for God's patience?
- In what way would I most like to grow more like God?

Some words to pray

Loving Father, I'm sorry for times when I get angry
for the wrong reasons.
I know it's right to be angry about some things,
because Jesus got angry
when people stopped others from coming to You.
Please help me to know when it's right to be angry,
and when it's wrong.
Please help me to talk to You about my anger
so I don't become bitter.
The Bible tells me You ARE love, and love is patient and kind.
Love doesn't bear a grudge and it never gives up.
Please help me to be more like You.
I need help to live for You,
so please fill me with Your Holy Spirit.
I ask these things in Jesus' name,
for my good and for Your glory. Amen.

Day 25   God's visual aid

Jonah 4 verses 6-8

6   Then the LORD God sent a leafy plant

and made it grow up over Jonah.

It gave him more shade for his head.

It made him more comfortable.

Jonah was very happy he had the leafy plant.

7   But before sunrise the next day, God sent a worm.

It chewed the plant so much that it dried up.

8   When the sun rose, God sent a burning east wind.

The sun beat down on Jonah's head.

It made him very weak. He wanted to die.

So he said, "I'd rather die than live."

Some things to notice

God didn't argue with Jonah when he sulked.

He gave him a visual aid to show him what was going on.

God provided a leafy plant for a shelter

and Jonah was really happy.

Then God sent a worm to eat the plant so it dried up.

Then God turned the heat up on Jonah.

Jonah didn't like it.

He thought death would be better than putting up with it.

In the next session we will discover why God sent the plant.

Some questions to think about

- Can I think of another time in the Bible
  when God used a picture or a story
  to help someone understand?
  Why are they sometimes more helpful
  than a regular explanation?
- Do I get too easily upset when things change,
  so that I'm happy one minute and sad the next?
- What truths about God could help me
  when I'm grumpy?

Some words to pray

Loving Father, thank You that You always know
the best way to handle people.
I don't always know what to do.
Please give me wisdom when my friends and family
or people I work with are grumpy or sulky.
Please give me good ideas about how to respond.
Thank You for the times You have shown me truth gently.
I'm sorry for the times when I'm sulky or cranky.
I need help to live for You,
so please fill me with Your Holy Spirit.
I ask these things in Jesus' name,
for my good and for Your glory. Amen.

Day 26   Jonah's heart

Jonah 4 verses 9-10

9   God said, "Is it right for you to be angry
    about the plant?"

    "It is," Jonah said.

    "In fact, I'm so angry I wish I were dead."

10 But the Lord said,

    "You have been concerned about this plant.

    But you did not take care of it.

    You did not make it grow.

    It grew up in one night and died the next."

Some things to notice

God began to show Jonah the root of his anger.

He uncovered the truth about Jonah's heart.

Jonah didn't make the plant or look after it.

Yet he didn't want God to destroy it.

This was very different to Jonah's attitude to Nineveh!

He wanted God to destroy the people there.

Jonah's anger showed he only really cared about himself.

He cared about the plant

more than he cared about all those people—

people whom God loved.

Ouch! Truth can hurt. Truth can also set us free!

Some questions to think about

- What things upset me and make me angry?
- What does that tell me about my heart?
  What does it say about what I care about most?
- Do I want God to help me change?

Some words to pray

Loving Father, the truth can be painful.

Jesus said that the truth will set me free.

It's scary, but I ask You to show me the truth about my heart.

Please show me gently. Please help me to accept the truth.

Please help me to want to change.

I can't change myself. I need Your help.

Please fill me afresh with Your Holy Spirit.

I ask these things in Jesus' name,

for my good and for Your glory. Amen.

Day 27   God's heart

In today's passage, God is speaking to Jonah.

Jonah 4 verse 11

11   "And shouldn't I show concern
for the great city of Nineveh?
It has more than 120,000 people.
They can't tell right from wrong.
Nineveh also has a lot of animals."

Some things to notice

God knew the number of people in Nineveh.

God made them. God cared for each one.

He knew their hearts, just like He knew Jonah's heart.

God even cared for the animals in Nineveh.

He made all of them.

Jonah cared about the plant even though he hadn't made it.

God cared even more about the people in Nineveh

because he did make them!

God asked Jonah,

"Shouldn't I show concern for ... Nineveh?"

We don't have Jonah's answer.

The question God asked Jonah is left open.

God wants us to ask ourselves that question.

Some questions to think about

- Am I more like Jonah or more like God in this story?
- Are there people who are in trouble
  who I don't particularly like
  or who I just don't know very well?
  What does God think about them?
  What can I pray for them?
- Are there people God has given me a love for,
  who don't know Him? How will I pray for them
  and show them He loves them?

Some words to pray

Loving Father, thank You that Your love is for everyone
and You want all people to know You as Saviour and Lord.
Please give me a concern for others and a heart like Yours.
Help me to think like You think.
There are so many people in need around the world.
There are too many for me to think about.
Please would You show me who and what to pray for today.
I need help to live for You,
so please fill me with Your Holy Spirit.
I ask these things in Jesus' name,
for my good and for Your glory. Amen.

Day 28   The big picture

Recap: Jonah 4 verse 2

2   He prayed to the LORD.

Here is what Jonah said to him.

"LORD, isn't this exactly what I thought would happen

when I was still at home?

That is what I tried to prevent

by running away to Tarshish.

I knew that you are gracious. You are tender and kind.

You are slow to get angry. You are full of love.

You are a God who takes pity on people.

You don't want to destroy them."

 ### Some things to notice

Jonah always knew what God is like.

God is kind and full of grace and mercy.

Jonah relied on God's kindness.

God hates sin: he has said that the penalty for sin is death.

Yet God would rather save than destroy.

He gives people a chance to change.

Jonah wasn't anything like God!

Some questions to think about

- How sure am I about what God is like?
- Do I think God did the right thing
  in not destroying the Ninevites?
- How can God forgive sin and still be just (fair)?

The answer to the last question leads us
to look at God's Son, Jesus.
We'll look at Jesus in the next 2 studies.
It's only through Jesus' life, death and resurrection
that God can forgive sin without being unjust.
Jesus took the punishment for all our sin.
Sin is punished, but sinners are forgiven.

 Some words to pray

Loving Father,
thank You that You are always kind and ready to forgive.
Thank You that You are also fair and just.
I'm sorry for when I hold on to grudges
and won't forgive others.
Thank You that because of Jesus I can know
Your goodness and Your forgiveness.
Please help me to be more like You today.
I need help to live for You,
so please fill me with Your Holy Spirit.
I ask these things in Jesus' name,
for my good and for Your glory. Amen.

Day 29 — Another prophet from Galilee

What's going on?

Many people were saying that Jesus was not from God.
They said he was a liar.

John 7 verses 50-52

50 Then Nicodemus, a Pharisee, spoke.

He was the one who had gone to Jesus earlier.

He asked,

51 "Does our law find a man guilty

without hearing him first?

Doesn't it want to find out what he is doing?"

52 They replied, "Are you from Galilee too?

Look into it. You will find that a prophet does not

come out of Galilee."

More info

Pharisees were an ancient Jewish group.
They were very religious and kept lots of rules.
Some of them were God's rules and some were not.
A prophet is someone who has been sent by God
with a message for people. Jesus was a prophet,
but he was also much more than a prophet!

Some things to notice

Nicodemus was a Pharisee. He believed

that Jesus was God's promised Messiah (Saviour and King).

He wanted to persuade the other Pharisees to listen to Jesus.

But they said that no prophet came from Galilee.

Jesus came from Galilee.

So, they could not believe that Jesus was the Messiah.

The Pharisees thought they knew the Scriptures

better than anyone else.

But they forgot that *Jonah* was a prophet

who came from Galilee!

 Some questions to think about

- Have I got fixed ideas about Jesus?
  Are they based on the Bible or just what I think?
- What things do people I know believe about Jesus?
  What truths about him have they missed?
- Do I stand up for Jesus like Nicodemus did?

 Some words to pray

Loving Father,

thank You that You have shown us who You are in the Bible.

Please help my friends and family understand who Jesus is.

Please help me today to be like Nicodemus

and to stand up for what's true, even if it's not easy.

I ask these things in Jesus' name,

for my good and for Your glory. Amen.

Jesus and Jonah

 ## What's going on?

Just before these verses, Jesus healed lots of people.

Jesus healed a blind, dumb, demon-possessed man.

The Pharisees said the devil gave Jesus the power to do that.

They didn't think these signs were big enough

to show that Jesus was God's promised Messiah.

So they asked for a different sign.

Matthew 12 verses 38-40

38 Some of the Pharisees and the teachers of the law

   came to Jesus. They said,

   "Teacher, we want to see a sign from you."

39 He answered,

   "Evil and unfaithful people ask for a sign!

   But none will be given

   except the sign of the prophet Jonah.

40 Jonah was in the belly of a huge fish

   for three days and three nights.

   Something like that will happen to the Son of Man.

   He will spend three days and three nights in the grave."

Some things to notice

The Pharisees forgot about Jonah before,

so Jesus reminded them.

Jonah didn't die in the fish. He came out alive.

Jesus WAS going to die,

but 3 days later He would rise again!

This is the best sign of all of God's goodness and power.

Jesus' death and resurrection were a "Jonah" sign.

Some questions to think about

- What have I seen Jesus do in my life
  or the lives of others?
- Am I ever tempted to ask Jesus for a sign? When? Why?
- What do Jesus' death and resurrection tell me
  about who Jesus is and about what God is like?
- Is that enough of a sign for me?

Some words to pray

Loving Father, thank You for being at work in my life.

Thank You for Your work in the lives of others.

I'm sorry for when I'm jealous and compare myself to others.

Please help me to see more clearly what You are doing.

I'm sorry when I don't notice and don't praise You.

Please help me to show people that Jesus is my Saviour

by the things I say and do.

I need help to live for You,

so please fill me with Your Holy Spirit.

I ask these things in Jesus' name,

for my good and for Your glory. Amen.

My thoughts and questions

My prayers and answers to prayer

Now explore the life of Jesus!

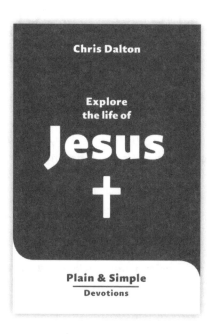

30 short chapters to help you get to know Jesus better

COMPANY

BIBLICAL | RELEVANT | ACCESSIBLE

At The Good Book Company we are dedicated to helping Christians and local churches grow. We believe that God's growth process always starts with hearing clearly what he has said to us through his timeless and flawless word—the Bible.

Ever since we opened our doors in 1991, we have been striving to produce resources that are biblical, relevant, and accessible. By God's grace, we have grown to become an international publisher, encouraging ordinary Christians of every age and stage and every background and denomination to live for Christ day by day and equipping churches to grow in their knowledge of God, their love for one another, and the effectiveness of their outreach.

Call one of our friendly team for a discussion of your needs or visit one of our local websites for more information on the resources and services we provide.

Your friends at The Good Book Company

thegoodbook.com | thegoodbook.co.uk
thegoodbook.com.au | thegoodbook.co.nz